Your Kingdom

Also by Eleni Sikelianos

From Coffee House Press:

Earliest Worlds (2001)

The California Poem (2004)

Body Clock (2008)

The Loving Detail of the Living & the Dead (2013)

You Animal Machine (2014)

Make Yourself Happy (2017)

From Other Presses:

to speak while dreaming (Selva Editions, 1993)

The Book of Tendons (The Post-Apollo Press, 1997)

The Monster Lives of Boys and Girls
        (Green Integer, National Poetry Series Prize, 2003)

The Book of Jon (City Lights, 2004)

What I Knew (Nightboat Books, 2019)

Praise for Eleni Sikelianos

"This is writing and reading as adventure, where every page can bring a different sort of revelation." —*Kirkus,* **starred review**

"Sikelianos's poems collect the world and then disassemble it. They prove her to be one of our most free-thinking and innovative poets, whose evolving work continually challenges the boundaries of her art while retaining an essential lyricism." —**Carol Moldaw,** *Boston Review*

"Electric as a lightning storm, wild as a first-growth forest, protean as fantasy's shape-shifters—that's Sikelianos's poetry, a real pleasure to read." —*Library Journal*

"Eleni Sikelianos is the vagabond traveler dreaming Sappho's words in the desolate lands . . . to reveal Poetry as a secret way of knowing." —**Cecilia Vicuña**

"Whether Sikelianos is writing about making a paper globe, making a family, making a statement, or making yourself, she surveys the field of human endeavors to find new prospects for care amid precarious political contexts." —**Srikanth Reddy,** *BOMB Magazine*

"I turn to Eleni Sikelianos's poems when the drastic gracelessness of capital has me in gridlock." —**Lisa Roberston**

"Sikelianos's voice is unmistakable, and her poetic continuance of the observant, the ethical, and the oracular awake is in vital presence." —*EOAGH*

"[Sikelianos] is a voice, or voices, unlike anything in contemporary poetry." —**John Ashbery**

"[A] miraculous poet." —**Anne Waldman**

"So she does what only a master poet can do—discovers the world once again." —**Robert Creeley**

"An original and beautiful poetry, always discovering its own grammar and name, its own secrets. The poetry comes from her and not others: it is incomparable."   **—Alice Notley**

"Sikelianos directs us, surprise in each line, to return to the unconscious, to the fierce, absolute sign, out of whose nourishing hand her poetry advances."   **—Barbara Guest**

"Eleni's language—body-language, breath, and babies' many minds behind—a poem that won't let you go 'til it's done with you, its sinuous whipping lines."   **—Gary Snyder**

"This text is one-of-a-kind . . . writing itself in vision-meters, jagged, fearless new languages, and thought-arrangements for us to enter and un-peel the incredible life-life-is."   **—Juan Felipe Herrera**

"The real and the imagined, waking life and dream, the simple and the complex . . . work together and play together in Eleni Sikelianos's poetry with a wonderful elasticity and verve."   **—Lydia Davis**

"Sikelianos is a shamanistic denizen of the desert and the dark, but her journey is laced with irony as well as wisdom and beauty—expect lazurite to coexist with KFC bones stuffed under a mattress, expect a narrator as tough and hard-assed as her fascinating, fugitive subject."   **—Maggie Nelson**

"With her native Greek wisdom and her American exuberance, Eleni takes us into the different layers which make our daily lives, perceptions, thoughts . . . as they take form, and thanks to her become an initiatique, even archeological, journey."   **—Etel Adnan**

"[Sikelianos is] responding to the tradition of American epic and enlarging its 'we.' . . . Just gorgeous."   **—Solmaz Sharif**

"Like only the best poets, Sikelianos leaves us changed from how we thought we knew our world."   **—CA Conrad**

Your Kingdom

Eleni Sikelianos

COFFEE HOUSE PRESS

Minneapolis

2023

Coffee House Press books are available to the trade through our primary distributor, Consortium Book Sales & Distribution, cbsd.com or (800) 283-3572. For personal orders, catalogs, or other information, write to info@coffeehousepress.org.

Coffee House Press is a nonprofit literary publishing house. Support from private foundations, corporate giving programs, government programs, and generous individuals helps make the publication of our books possible. We gratefully acknowledge their support in detail in the back of this book.

Library of Congress Cataloging-in-Publication Data

Names: Sikelianos, Eleni, author.
Title: Your kingdom / Eleni Sikelianos.
Description: [Minneapolis] : Coffee House Press, 2023.
Identifiers: LCCN 2022032055 (print) | LCCN 2022032056 (ebook) | ISBN
    9781566896597 (paperback) | ISBN 9781566896603 (epub)
Subjects: LCGFT: Poetry.
Classification: LCC PS3569.I4128 Y68 2023 (print) | LCC PS3569.I4128
    (ebook) | DDC 811/.54--dc23/eng/20220711
LC record available at https://lccn.loc.gov/2022032055
LC ebook record available at https://lccn.loc.gov/2022032056

Printed in the United States of America

30 29 28 27 26 25 24 23   1 2 3 4 5 6 7 8

All life love[s] itself

Contents

Bestiaries on the Lamb

All the Living Living Together (Reevolutionize)

Chemical Kisses

Deevolutionize

Blind lady in the storm tapping

the snowbank

with her red-tipped stick, a stiff, slender

ticking tongue

I saw it and asked Siri

to write that down

From the backseat Maggie said

Why can't your mom write

Because she's driving, says daughter

Watch what you say

She's a poet

She takes notes

"Nothing in evolution makes sense except in the light of phylogeny" (Notes)

One July, among the California redwoods, I watched a fire-colored salamander lumber over a log, and so my mind was ignited to meditate on shoulder girdles. Amphibians invented them.

In the mid-nineteenth century the German biologist Ernst Haeckel coined the term *phylogeny* to contain the notion of the organismal lineages we all passed through. You too may have admired the drawings of diatoms, shells, jellyfish, radiolarians, and spiders he sketched to describe life on earth.

 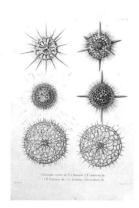 

phyla (φυλή):

    tribe, stem, branch

                                                  geny (γεν):

                                                  born, birth.

Phylogeny: all the plants who grew to be you. All the animals who did. I don't mean because you were the *telos causa*, the reason or end result, and I don't mean because you ate them. I mean because they invented earth. Eventually they also invented you.

They twisted and turned and licked and hissed and allowed you to exist.

Phylogeny, a word I loved, was invented by a man who believed in *eugenics* (a word in turn invented by a man who invented *nature vs. nurture*).

eu (ευ): good, well   *geny* (γεν): birth, born.

Ecology, phylum, Protista

are also words first made in Haeckel's mounding mouth.

Here I am at the bottom of Haeckel's *World-Riddle*. Every word I utter

haunted. In conflict with all the animals.

Can anything ever be held away from human tongues?

Some hunters, in ritual, sidewaysed the names

for bears (*arktos, ursus*), a

taboo on naming what is wild.

Instead of *bear*, a hunter said *the brown one; honey-eater; good-calf; honey-pig.*

As soon as a bear

crept out of a word, a word

did its work

to erase the bear.

The animals' names light up in crackling flames.

Names mane & unmane.

Now we were rolling around on earth draping our tongues in Latin things.

We always said the bird doesn't care what you call it.

That's one way I'm different from a bird.

                                          The bird takes flight from its

word.

We all passed through roots and branches of the same tree, beginning somewhere with a few molecules combusting.

You share 70% of your DNA with zebrafish.

In the '60s biologist Lynn Margulis reshowed us symbiogenesis: we came about not only through competition but through lavish, revolutionary conviviality. We carry evidence of species merger in our cells, and of species relation in almost every structure we daily rely upon.

Organismal lineages veering orgasmal.

                                         One gene sliding into another one.

Is there one piece of you that doesn't also, in some form, belong to someone else?

Your fingers ghosting chimp as they slender through air.

Orangutan echo around the mouth.

Lobe-finned fishes did protolungs; acorn worms, something like a heart; amphibians, we've said, did shoulders. The more complex organs, like eyes, had to be developed many times, but jellyfish saw first, and not for us.

I live on Earth at present I don't know what I am.

I seem to be a verb . . .

I swerve:

You know that science metaphors matter.

The physicist I sat next to at dinner in November[1] was upset that the sound of two black holes colliding, captured by

> *a pair of delicately positioned mirrors [tracking] the squeezing and stretching of space as gravitational waves go by*

was metaphored into an unsightly sound.

Black holes utter no thing heard by humans.

But now your ears hear beastish heavy breathing at your night door, a monster with a liquid heart monitor on. The deep water of dark space. This silent sound is ancient, and the energy it unleashed was fifty times greater than all observable stars.

[go to: sound of "black holes colliding"]

Margulis took issue with Darwin's adopted tree image. No! she says, unless a tree has liquid, dripping branches. But a net, yes, because everyone is and was sharing everything all the time, sliding intimate materials between us, sucking off the same mouth of invention. It's a man-made metaphor, and she can make a woman one.

My physicist says only math is not metaphoric. Language itself, which includes numbers, heaves to carry meaning from there (deep space) to here (you; hello).

Biology, like language, is remembering. What life *is* is your cells remembering what other life did before it.

And even further.

----

1 S. James Gates

Our cells recall ancient chemical joys and traumas, pre-life, while our limbs remember salamanders. A poem remembers our past in language and posits a future in the simplest sense, like a to-do note, hoping that it will be seen at some point hence and remind us of something worth knowing, feeling. It is an ecosystem that, like any functioning system, should deal with its own shit.

If we let *phyla* be taken over by its bedmate and homonym, *phylla* (leaves, petals, sprouts, sheaves, sheets of paper), we clear a silent space where we are all bound together and leafing from the same roots. If we take it further, to its homonymic neighbor, *philo*, we fall into love, with all our living friends, and with the dead left in traces

       under oceans and in rivers and lake beds

In the beginning

there was no doom.

The large grass-eating mammals were absent and so were the grasslands

for them to feed upon. Rodents and seed-eating birds, the rose-crowned fruit dove

and carunculated caracara, no. The great burgeoning of flowering plants had

not yet taken place. So no bees, no. Corals had arisen and corals had exited.

Hard-hooved animals with grain-crushing molars had not arrived, nor had
the carnivores with meat-ripping incisors to eat them. No hooves left over
in the field. No fridge-sized elephant seals bodyslamming on the beach nor
amphibian intestines. Obviously no Christmas, and no

Christmas-tree worms had yet extended their feathery plumes

and delicate radioles for trapping

scraps of food. No to party politics. Yes to genetic drift. In this picture,
your ancestors are shadowy creatures. (We'll get back to you when more
fossil data becomes available.)

So,

person, what

next?   What if,   what if we saved it

all, friend?

"I leave the word 'saved' to let the pattern speak"

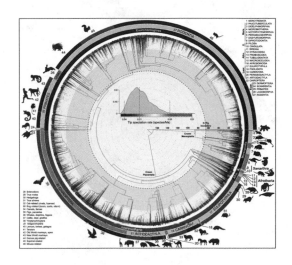

At all hours our bodies

Sketch around us

Immense

Immense overlapping circles

Of the footprints of beasts

—*Eléni Vakaló*

In the Museum of Comparative Anatomy

(That's How Dumb You Are)

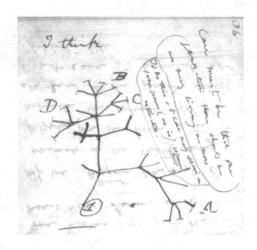

Ruins are relics.

The lineage being of little importance, we're

related to them.

—Etel Adnan

In the Great Hall of Bones

    (at the Musée d'Anatomie Comparée)

The face like a magnet draws to itself

animal parts

       rabbit paw

       veal gut

       pig light

to the eye & the skin & the teeth & the tongue

to echo the chaos of mouth

more crumpled mammal than

       daylight

As when moons have moons

your kisser a satellite

to talk (a kind of traffic) attracting

       words

which hover at the lip trying

to describe or define

     the first plants

     last elephant or

what resides deep

in the heart, daughter

if you ask

Where do hearts come from?

I'll say

your ticker too is daughter

to a turtle's who got it

off bacteria

and in turn

in the Great Hall of Bones tell me

a gibbon's skull

doesn't look like yours or mine

I mistake your foot

for a flipper

your tongue for an ascidian

sea squirt

Whose newborn skull is that

some other you put in the window?

Human, chimp, orangutan, gorilla?

The you splits in two, pluralizing

toward a we, and we have no trouble

displaying stuffed bonobos and gibbons

but usually (not always) draw the line at *sapiens*. Should your mirror

self wish to compare

a flamingo's liver to a toucan's, a ray's, or a buzzard's

a fox's stomach

to an ox's bladder

an elephant's esophagus to a gazelle's

you've put them all here

in jars lining the walls with light

pouring through just

as it pours through the skeletons once the flesh

is removed. The rib rings what's right

in us while the eye

rings what's wrong. What's wrong? In tongues, you have

seals, panthers, black bears, hyenas

lions, anteaters, peccaries, llamas

coatis and the black-and-white ruffed lemur of Madagascar, for starters

each in their glass flask

floating in yellow elixir. What ancient

witch's chamber is this that houses, superstitious, a

giraffe's rumpled *papilles du palais*, a palace

where taste no longer takes place?

You were sure a giraffe never used such a thing to talk

You said, Stay silent as a giraffe

I once pitched my tent in savannah grass and woke

into a sea of giraffe—did I hear their low muttering heart-night moans

like hearing a tenderized earthquake from underground at dawn?

This is your inner oracle speaking

(sound track: a bear's deep hibernation breathing):

and in the night you hear the bear

beget the bear, the fox be-

get the fox all

the social animals drink at the brook

Bird: is it a toy?

It shows us the limits

of what we can know

In the realm of blind pouches

(called ceca) you've collected

an eagle's, pheasant's, alpaca's, guanaco's

and you ascertain that a chimp's looks like a big mandrake root, which will scream

when yanked

from earth

We won't speak about what you've gathered in pancreases, lungs, branchies

but among the many hearts along the northwest wall I see

a harbor porpoise

crocodile

tortoise

python

I am looking at these skeletons thinking about myself—the thin

reflection in the glass where over

the incredible architectural curve of some spine I see

my eyes are puffy from too much wine and

some you's blue

tennis shoes—

In my mind I animate

the one-eyed pig, the two-headed snake, the necessity

     to learn how to lean

into each

        other & breathe

and I am sweating a lot by now in the hall

all these organs have lost their use and color, swimming in ancient alcohol and

I ran out of time before I could note them all, but saw

further on, a tiny little dried-up human brain looks like an overgrown acorn

That's how dumb you are.

lacrimal bone

I wish to speak of

the smallest, most fragile fragment

of the face, floating

in orbital space roughly

the size of your little fingernail near

the eye-corner, its bony

landmarks

help you to

cry

when you've lost your lover

    mother

    father

in the night

heart's vapor rises to the head

flicks some speck of brain

the crying eye's arrow

true as a ray of the sun tipped with a photon

shoots out

and you think

whatever folly you plot, the world

will perform it

so

overblooming with us

but I don't want to leave you

here on earth with its geometrized urban

and agricultural cuts—give the map on your face

straight

correlation with the heliacal luminosity

of uncontaminable space—if you look up

Not Verb, but Vertigo

      (after Alejandra Pizarnik)

A yellow scraping across my skin when

I write the word *sky*

Not sky but scything :

    to let day be scraped out

        by night

I scratched down the word *flower* & felt

  the parts draw away from the page.

    Not *gnomon*, nor grown*man, but ghost :

      to gnaw on the crisp

            skin once it's been stripped down

       from the meat

       the neat meat

hiding under the table

of the skin's

tablatures

right at the juncture where day/night meet

you can see it indicated by the perforated lines

what parts of us don't cast a shadow

Wrong

I want to be wrong all day long.

As wrong as flesh machines.
No fact checker, no search it.
No it and no that.

I want to put my money in all the wrong places.
Misrecognize the most famous faces.

Tell me what

               leaf

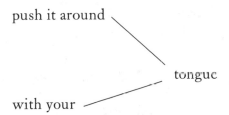

push it around

                    tongue

with your

Tell me what

                          -dom

free or king

domed out

above us &

hard to reach

Break the lid of it.
Don't tell me what it.

Tooth to Bite

First I got a tooth to bite you with

then you got a claw to smash me.

I got a horn to impale you

and you got a tusk to gore me.

I got a claw to sink into your spine

and you got spines to blow into mine.

I got a beak to stab your liver—

you got a talon to grab me by the cheek.

I got a poison stinger to stun you—

you, an alkaloid skin to fry me if I licked.

I went all flamboyant and shimmered in the sun to show how toxic I was;

you made a water pistol with your lips, snagged me

neat from ethers.

I got a black goo to choke your gills if you tried to bite and you

took on poison-filled exploding mandibular glands to guard your infantry.

You made your body into a battery and discharged 600 volts into our mutual estuary.

I said O.K., deadly mortal friend, I don't need to bite you, you don't need to roast me.

Then I got a gun and you

you showed up on the horizon with your nuclear weapons.

the tangled bank

slept synonyms
through the night

shouted regret in
kitchens

suspended consciousness
by which the body

stands, rests
and drops

darkness
into waters below

all your
shuteye

will give you this

face in utter darkness, crying
with total dedication

wantonly, with abandon

laughing into

a feeling of depth

I was thinking

thoughts don't think

my change

and then, yet, yes

daytime light through a barrel of trees

b/t the leaf & the tree

    b/t a they and a we

b/t the honey & the bee

    ands inch an ant along the counter

        stitching the diff

and this flower's shape will remember

        its sheath-tongued bee

      :

yes, of course the orchid

  /& its stamen/ will remember

   their lost bee

      :

bee orchid orchid bee

      :

by /lost/ we mean forever

by /remember/ we mean

what language traces of this

ravaging / see

Real World Feeds

All you who feed

on the food of earth

frog

like a piece of dry leather creaking   in the field

snapping up flies

hunter

licking the pot   of tiger bone stew

tire

  a black tongue lapping

a black cold road

Get this ghost mama off a me

What is it?

Looking for all the animals in their animal holes

You

a citadel of real cellular transparency

tangling an uncertain analogy between a lynx's and your own

                                    folded, sleeping limbs

       your gams and

       pinions and fins   like the mind: a mild or wild

       snarl   of yarn

Return all the soft-bodied animals

                 to their homes: *sea pansies, anemones*

          boars, bears

     even *pet guinea pigs* not distracted from being by

                     footsteps across the floor

We find ourselves cool and clean and

         in the next hour

you're in the night-surf, a ragged white washcloth stuffed in the corpse-mouth

ash-grey legs, wiry hairs nubbed down

        what animal cadaver

do you carry

the air there

outside your window

is around

       the tree

    I still

care for it, all

you   who

                    light-fingered

                       night-fingered

feed

:

paradise
before we
killed or
breathed

all my animal family

we are awakening and suffering together

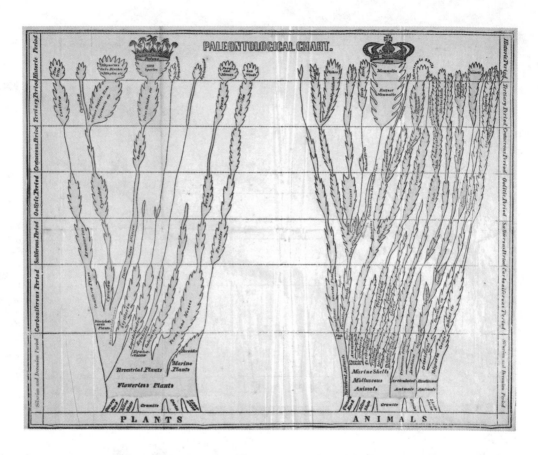

so by generation I believe it has been with the great Tree of Life, which fills with its [deep] and broken branches the crust of the earth, and covers the surface with its ever-branching and beautiful ramifications

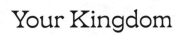

Your Kingdom

if you like let the body feel

        all its own evolution

        inside, opening flagella

& feathers & fingers

        door by door, a ragged

        neuron dangling like a

participle to

        hear a bare sound

        on the path, find

a red-eye-

hole rabbit, fat

of the bulbous stalk pecked out

        to the core (a

raptor did that)   so you can

bore back to the salamander you

                       once were straggling under the skin

grope

                              toward the protozoa

                  snagging on the rise toward placental knowing

       who developed eyes "for you" agape in open waters

the worm that made a kidney-like chamber burrows in

directing your heart leftward in nodal cascade, slow at your

              hagfish spine who

                  will bury your bones

               investigate a redwood rain or tap

             the garnet of your heartwood, bark? put

          your flat needles on dry ice to inquire

after your tree family, father or mother in the fairy-ring

         next to you, find you

are most closely related to grass

            (if you are a redwood)

your hexaploid breathing pores gently closing at night, when did you begin your coexistence with flowering

                          plants from which arose the bee before the

African honey badger but after the dark

protoplanetary disk of dust grains

               surrounding the sun become

                  the earth you

             had no nouns, did you

              feel the gravitational sorting in the

pre-lung graphite as it marked toward tissue, the split in

            prokaryotes when ether lipids did you

no good but still you learned to unleash

energy breaking/making bonds and house some ancient

          groping grains in your gut foraging on gases and

             who knows what

phototrophic algae did karate-chopping watersplitting

to feed on sunlight and thus you can

eat an apple after bacon benefiting

from the invention of glucose storage but

       the rugged sex life of the hermaphroditic banana slug, nipping

      at its partner's current penis (later, it's a vagina) in liquid crystal slime

has little to do with you yet you

can watch it and wonder at the structure

of your own snot's likeness to its plural wetnesses

now that you have learned to traffic

phonemes + genes in their own bio

chassis delivery system, glottal stop

in your *ci-ty* or *bu-tton* made possible by

obstructed airflow, when your organs made

for eating, breathing began to cry out, the tongue

in torsion to express your thought and

it was strange, how you altered

your formant frequencies, an [i] becomes a [u], around

the fire you switch to pure sound in the dark

and I know what you mean

Turn out the lights and say these words

[love]

[herd]

[draught]

[furred]

then draw them on the board

[behold, a thought-flower]

"no vocally impaired whale, dolphin

or [ ]bird . . . could express its song . . . in

visual display" you say (forgetting

a body breaching, spouting, winging is

its own author/ship). Yet matter is still

sometimes deaf to your summoning, metal

filings that won't cohere or the quantal sounds

of a photon can't

be convened

to your mind where what

flashes may be your

protoreptilian hind

brain, what you

learned from lizards gathered:

*   *   *   *   *   *   *   *   *   *   *

to sleep   to swallow   to hear   to see   to feel   even to dream   and later

*   *   *   *   *   *   *   *   *   *   *

you lost your wet snout as you moved

                          toward daylight, wax

        of the world made malleable as you reach

                              to touch it

your face a footnote

          to when you were swimming mouthfirst to taste

                      and test what was there because soon

you needed a head to see and hear your food

        *   *   *   *   *   *   *   *   *   *   *   *   *

someone had dropped the exoskeleton

like a weight into deep water plummeting

toward your dark vertebral lineage in blue

                      (could you even see that color?) and now

            you could bend with ease in each direction

        *   *   *   *   *   *   *   *   *   *   *   *   *

your fine-tuned tongue and auditory equipment bristling

        *   *   *   *   *   *   *   *   *   *   *   *   *

you arrange your syllables like a flock

of self-forming starlings in a draft aimed out

your mouth and at an ear—there is

another here—you see the dim

traceries of human faces,   charcoal in a night chamber
or so pale

                a pupil could not find such a pearl
in a milk pool and other warm & golden hues   as the tone
world presents itself as sculpted and so you rise

           to greet it, sing, around the time
tight patches of photoreceptors amass

             into the absurdity of eyes which have to develop
fifty, a hundred times, and generally birds

                 do it better than you, you

stumble at the gate with the sharks
a photon hits an opsin and trips

            a switch and you learn to bend the light, transparent

              crystallins clump like jelly and it
  goes opaque—were you

              supposed to keep those feathers?

               if not for flight, why?

        *   *   *   *   *

evolution rips

a scar across your

                    spine—the vertebrae spread

            so you can lift yourself and

                  step, but

                        too quick—

your ankle torques at concrete edges on your way to work, breaks, backbone

density defunct in your rush

                  to stand, so you try to uncouple

yourself from apes to keep a place

                  for the soul   like gelatin in

                  a saline solution

"SOUL HAS WEIGHT, PHYSICIAN THINKS"

                              And

WHERE DO YOU FALL

IN HUMAN-ANIMAL DIVIDE?

"WHO MOST BEARS THE ANIMAL BURDEN?"

And

HUMAN SOUL HAS

NO WINGS

BUT FLIES

You cannot

contain survival

& descent, integration & forgetfulness

in one untamed brain

extinction is a central feature of your model

you went wild with it

in just one shipwreck wiped out

an island's thrush, gerygone, fantail, starling, robust white-eye, plus

lizards, land snails, beetles

*   *   *   *   *   *   *   *

Worms could tell us about dirt

Birds could tell us about air

Ants about leaves

Leaves of light

Branches: wind and density

Orcas, the world and water

Seeds, of fire

*   *   *   *   *   *   *   *   *

Does seeing the flea magnified magnify the flea?

*   *   *   *   *   *   *   *   *   *   *

Consider the *e* in *motion*, the mouse

whose skull is cut out to show its acts of empathy

the prairie dog's jump-yip semaphore: *big   dog   yellow   fast*

     human   small   blue   slow

to warn its town of you

you were driving along a road in Colorado, the rocks were talking dinosaur

tracks across the Purgatoire Valley and so

   you find yourself in a crux of time, connected by memory

        to the past which

          is the world

           or

to the world, which is the past, and the shape

        of the future went weirder than ever

a sow is now

        growing your forthcoming heart

like a ghost organ eavesdropping on the teen pig's murmuring chambers

"I am listening to the salt inside your hunger" and it sounds

        like ether on silk

        spectral, velvet

        like a fingernail scraped along a vein

you were once an oceanaut in open waters in your own

private capsule, living in star-shaped structures (centuries), riding

        deep

        beneath the waves, rising

        up for air

     *   *   *   *   *   *   *   *   *   *   *

and now lying on the table you are

massaging the animals out of hiding; circling

your arm, bones rasp in the shoulder socket: pterodactyl

        wings unfolding from a locket

  you dig

        knuckles into gristle at the

  hip and a hare's

        tatter-

      demalion grey velvet

                                        ears unfurl

        from your inner thigh or

            some small synapsid

        squeaks out your top-

                                    most cervical spine

    and "you come out of dangerous plesiosaurs"

    your middle ear exapted out of reptilian mandibles

    you and other mammals use for hearing what crocodiles do for tearing

    if not up from the august tenebrae

    and fenestra of the dark past with

                                elastic energy in the rib cage

    then down with

                            zygomatic skull bones

                        embroidered like brittle silk

            onto

                    air / the world

                            where

            some crows lost their caw

                their predator warning

                (their predators were gone)

and you lost some vowels

down in the bowels, the organ-chambers where meaning

rounds itself toward night

*   *   *   *   *   *   *

In the strata of the rock is recorded

some of your earlier story though some scraps of it

are lost, you read it

                  in ocean silt: it would have been better

to go hermaphroditic or

                      parthenogenetic but you adapt

to the instability of two-sexed

reproduction with

                    glee, warm-blooded and arisen

from the loving filament

endowed with the power of acquiring

new hard parts and finding

they can be fluid—WORLD WITHOUT END!—your wing bones

                        grow lighter, your legs

heavy and as you rise you wonder, "has the oyster necessary

notion of space"? its brain too

                  trembling in the same slime-light

            *   *   *   *   *   *   *   *

Some serpentine proteins slip, tap

a cell wall and the whole thing floods

with smell—is it

burnt bacon from the back room? no, you've

traipsed too far forward; slide back,

           silurian, on the paleomap, you've a whole world to explore,

       vertebrate, on land, after the rise

          of fishes when

       the lobe-fins gave you a gift—someone

stuck an air-bladder onto their throat for buoyancy urgently

        to rise and sink in water and soon

you gulped a patch of air and lifted—your struggle then was

       with the elements, breathing

       was the least barrier but in water your body

had been a weightless lucent bubble, gliding; as you slithered to land your liver

       threatened to rip

through belly flesh; at first you swayed

       side to side as if

       still in water (watch a lizard

       walk and you'll see it) all the pressure

         hoisted in your

shoulder joint; elbow and knee sprawl sideways in the mud—

even now you stride-bounce, head

                              bobbing like a bright birth-

                    day balloon wandering

          the earth because of knees turned forward and

                                        elbows back as if

you were still stretching between atmospheres; reach out for

                    an apple or a daughter to keep her

                    from falling, you'll recognize

your upper arm bone in

Eusthenopteron's pectoral fin

less reliably your

                              finger bones and wrist as you tap

your device thank frogs

                    for making you this plus

ears to hear in air   even if   phylogenetic difficulties arise

                              when you were a fish—how inconvenient—

                    if you bent your head

                    you also bent your body

oh! your neck! you can arch it independently, side-eye! someone

who crawled to land, flat-headed, made it

if in your fish life your hip girdle was

                      tiny and could float you had to

lock it down—some proto-newt reattached

the shoulder muscles from the skull to ribs for you

so that each step-shock

                            wouldn't slosh

                    your brains about—cuz on land

you were more prone to accidents, crashing

                              headlong into rocks

your teeth were like labyrinths then

this mattered to you later because labyrinthodonts arranged

skull-roofing bones to palace said brain for you

        *   *   *   *

and you go dizzy from the deep

                expanse of it—how to find yourself

in space in such an

animal carnival

        *   *   *   *

bats' wings worked over right through the centuries

insects snapped into being in lightning flashes

long-toed corncrakes living in meadows

a lens-shaped swelling: the crustacean's eye
excluding lateral pencils of light

the boy-bird ever in its bright nuptial plumage

the tiger's sharpened teeth agleam through trees

if green woodpeckers alone had existed
or the orange smolder of orangutans in forests

the tarsier's grand photon-sweeping eye in certain
symmetry with electromagnetic fields and
                                        spacetime

eels wielding at will all the "artillery of the skies"

the anxious bee around its aureole

head or umbel?

the adherent nectary gone quiet

stamen primordia, here is a gene for it

     each seed's sculptural catalogue and catastrophe,
       box elder samaras whirligigging, wings and

bodies in compressible flow

*   *   *   *   *   *   *   *   *   *   *

*   *   *   *   *   *   *   *   *   *   *

the columbiform

rose-crowned fruit dove

the curiquingue

nature-made

you named it

       ptilinopus regina   *carunculated caracara*

*   *   *   *   *   *   *   *   *   *   *

the velvet-antlered caribou in autumn pelage stamping

packed earth and an arctic fox's feet

in deep winter will keep from freezing

*   *   *   *   *   *   *   *   *

you have ingested many animals & arrested

       their outward movement

as the deer translates itself

                inside your flesh

you are rubbing up against this intimate enzymatic magic

transforming the shreds, super metaphoric

you can't start from scratch, can

only build with what others built before you

yet contra *Natura non facit saltum*[2]

you *can* jump! like an eruciform (*caterpillar*) does

to lepidopteran (*moth*), holing up in self-

made chambers, radically translating its own meat, squishy

      to wafery,

          dusted—

so some maggot ancestors engaged

          in gustatory or sexed hybridogenesis

           with lord-knows-who

      and invented metamorphosis out of several species—

      Saltatory! Salutations! New creatures!

    *   *   *   *   *   *   *   *   *   *   *

---

2 Nature makes no leap

the eagle will not describe to you

    ultraviolet's color array

    so you remain in the half-

light looking through your approximating eye which cannot

correct the aberrations of thought or light

in the fish-mirror you may trace with your finger

    on your embryo's neck the arteries' loop-like course

        : memento of the gills' former home

and the tiny hole near your brother's ear never closed, refusing

to disguise his amphibious beginnings

someone called it a preauricular sinus, someone

    named it a remnant, a rag

        a wormhole into

    the wet vestibules of time and space

do you recall—I remember

    the exact moment in the poolhall you recognized

the pattern on the leather armchair your own

                                        arm was draped across
each pinprick in your pored skins
a portal of relation, a webbed and reddened constellation
        count stars in the dark and stars in the day, are they
                separate electrical weights?

                *   *   *   *   *   *   *   *

you co-opted an egg sac's
folds for breathing or
a barnacle did it for you

as if each you was a metaphor for us

                                                did you note
                                                the diversity
                                                in shapes
                                        of birds' kidneys?
                        the snakes' specific swallowing?

                "the cartilaginous silence" around a shark?

                        compound curve in the adder's fang?

                                future color of your plumage?

                        *   *   *   *   *   *

the sky made wide enough for birds to wing it

*   *   *   *   *   *   *   *   *   *   *   *

what moved the glassy rock of earth toward greening

the bushes clothed and clotted, preening

you are not the only you to invent orchestration

all the syntax in mouse song sounding out some-
where between bird-syllable and your thumb scrubbing a glass clean

as you hum in the kitchen
and wipe the dishes

wellmet
wellmet

horse, wombat, whale, monkey

your truss root patches of color
your milk-fed young
your long-range genes proceeding out of time, a parade
of freighted squiggles translating themselves into teeth

*   *   *   *   *   *   *   *   *   *   *   *

now your bigger brain is awake with oxygen

please thank the bacteria who did the first work for you, prying hydro-

gen loose

so you could

        think &

breathe

doing what weird things

           with ropes and pulleys, or,

bathing your children, netting

pretend fish in the tub, manufacturing story

      my tables further show

            like some plants you are high

      on the organization scale which makes you

               wanton with some

lazy notion of perfection

but even viruses have fancier cloaking strategies

your work-shy genome straggling (all those do-

nothing nucleotides hanging around your DNA)

      still, "family is a pond to you"

        a place you bathe but forget your uncles

and you are clustered like a star-struck satellite with others

in your order

around forms

your unclawed manus

reaching toward a glass of wine

    which used to be a vine and you can

tie it, slice a peach, take a twig

       dip for ants

your forward-facing eye swims in a private puddle beside its neighbor so

on your night walk beside the lake you see

      dents in starlight when a planet passes

      pallid figures rise up

          from deep waters toward a mirrored surface

            breaking, rippling

      each cell and face the soul of itself bursting

    *   *   *   *   *   *   *   *   *   *   *

"What good is half a wing or half an eye? This point

will be taken up later" when you get to warring

and shredding each other apart, clearly

not all things are made for flight yet had you used

your incipient wing organs in air when they were fins

you might now flap hands and share

a flying squirrel's patagium, gliding

beech to beech

*   *   *   *   *   *   *   *   *   *   *

"My dear Darwin," you
too diversified from some hoary
      extinct form

you, a "wreck of ancient
    life," your front
      and hind legs homologous and
    little parts of you whittled like a
blade made for one exacting task

all these geological ages you've had
      to work on your tongue and hands! so you can
    pry open the oyster with your fingers
      and gulp, say

"snake knots" and "snack bots," "germ plasm spasm" with ease

    mouth writhing around the sounds
      of murder

    *   *   *   *   *

you chalk out upon a wall an antelope and give it legs

      as if you could run

         abreast of it along the cave

this is your first moving picture and you lie down

     beside it, all the previous

       &current species living in your

          veins snugged asleep inside you

           * * * * * * * * * * *

an infolding idiom in a curled up indri's and your drowsing limbs

           * * * * * * * * * * *

you've drawn a line for what is a circle

a tree for what is a tangled net

you've tried to structure or to rupture it

of course the chimp is cousin of your children

hear it scold in treetops and you'll know it

       grunt   wheeze   kiss   hum

         * * * * * * * * * * *

and of the bearded dragon lizard

    golden & long in

      slow-wave sleep

    hippocampal sharp-wave rippling *   *   *   *   *   *   *   *
*   *

the lizard is aura of geology, skinscape meta-

    phoric of metamorphic rocks, moving

    bits of neuronal playback around the brain, it does

      in 80 seconds what it takes you

      seven, eight hours to complete

your earholes and its: wormholes unclosable   over-open

    to empty space

                *   *   *   *   *

even sleep—you share it

        with invertebrates, who

      made it; a deep, dark den to enter

and lay the fray down, what fracas

         you can't use, put it

      in your sleep-cave, skin a golden scaling arched over

where you go dreaming full

bags of time

       & empty

bags of time

                flickering through the hours

the brimming bag of time is thick black sticky

                                      paste

      consistency of opium   stuck to the

       plastic bag of time slowing the real down   *   *

*   *   *   *   *

you are besotted with time's evidence in your own body

with each fresh day-decay

night's a new star now

                      how star

                   starry are you

              out in the sleeplands

very : the heaviest

                 bits of your body

are oldest megacosm stuff   (you knew that)

drifting past meteoric debris

tell

tell us time

in the sounding room

chant out

a self-song in the story time

*   *   *   *   *   *   *   *   *   *   *   *

Here is a story now.

Once, the sun-god's son

asked his father to prove his fathering

like you'd ask a word to prove its origin.

So, the old god let the boy drive his car, yellow

feathers lifting him

closer to the sun, but the boy

crashed straight into earth and singed it.

Look.

Both Poles are glowing. Once they go

Your palace is rubbish in space.

And you ask

unabashedly, if

EYE NOT CREATED

BY GOD

what

could save all this

if

anything will get us through it's

some

thing some

other BEING

broke off from the

ANIMAL-PLANT-SHROOM-VIRAL web-tree, maybe something

a bloodbelly comb jelly

invented and

you learn how to use it

can you do it

without destroying

all of us?   *   *   *   *   *   *   *   *   *   *   *   *

such are the facts

you made longer leg bones to chase, they made longer leg bones to run away each animal adds beauty in its evolutionary tricks   to hunt and to hide,

                              to allure, to protect, attract, make meals of

                                             to mate and to ride

                    waves   of   wild   energy

        *   *   *   *   *   *   *   *   *   *   *   *   *

so you wrap a feather shroud around you and lie down

or you

                        dress yourself in a lime-green macaw

cape still bright

long after

        the birds' sapphire and ventricle-red wing-

        explosion in air is over

                        carrying color forward in time and pressing it

close to the heart

                                of the matter: where

                                do you meet

bird, quill, fur? where

air?

last earth?

first water?

so you'll see this cell as it

                                        splits its sides

And you ask

am I made of answer

                                    in a small broken night

or of question in a big open light

                                        fairy-gauged

open as early dark

                            when the corpuscles of light

                                    dilate, get floppy

and the species is ready to crawl   stand   run

*   *   *   *   *   *   *   *   *   *   *   *   *

                                swim bladder : lung

                        branchiae, backscale : wing, wing-

cover

                                sponges : collagen; thus,

skin

                                comb jellies :

symmetry

                                cnidarians or sponges :

motility

                                             flatworms :

hunting   (?)

                                             shark's fin :

wrist

                                             zebrafish :

finger

your bones lulled in sand &

     lapped by rivers, lakes, and seas—

the gentler the better to later tell the story

       of what the world looked like when, and what

remains *weathering out* above the rock surface

found roadside : a

                                   marvelous   early   shoulder

*   *   *   *   *   *   *   *   *   *   *

* * * * * * * * * * * * * *

Little scenes of hunger, or love, or greed reshaping a hand or root.

Darkness bleeding into subarachnoid space.

* * * * * * * * * * * * *

No body plan   no mind to have it

turning in the fluids of some

                                                            "tiny

                                                      [wet] balloon"

A space, a future

                                                      body cavity

hunkering down in

                                                      fold holds

no sweet waltz yet

                                    —no sweat—

            just a deep   enormous

                                                      panthalassa

your mama

ocean

turning a gelatinous blob to nerve and bone — Oh!
a cell signaled to another — a kind of first talking

then some daughter did not separate

during division, deciding

it was better to stick together

That was in the mother of all

us others (Animals) ("Mama," after Ocean, being

Sponges)

So signaling started between non-related creatures "pressed

inward," the way you would now press your palms to your cheeks or your

tongue to your teeth

ancient gestures between one-celled beings   gathering *   *   *
*   *   *   *   *

Then

you started to bunch &

move & sprout & wriggle

  wheeze & creep, buzz

   or leap

soon one part of you could see

  & smell & feel & hear

another part of you could

  move & together you

    made an arc

  between the parts

  arc

         between

      the parts a

filament   trussing   thought

      cathedraling tissue   * * *

it's a wonder all your previous selves

  work together as you walk

   down Broadway!

 * * * * * * * *

I wanted to tell you

　　　　how you still have to carry

　　　　the sea around inside you

I mean you walked out of the ocean with ocean

　　　　keeping the percentages pretty straight

　*　　*　　*　　*　　*　　*　　*　　*　　*　　*　　*　　*　　*

what is that swirling sparking sparkling darkling

　　　　　　　　　　　　　　　cloud

　of blue up in your skull

　　　doing now?

　(I mean: an electrical storm became your brain)　*　　*　　*　　*　　*

Anyway, put Pennsylvania over

　　　your former Amazonia

　　throw Siberia on your prior desert as an icy blanket

　　Ohio over your ancient reefs

Soon, *the [N]ereids [will] roam astounded*

　　　Through submerged gardens,

　　　　Swim in silent wonder into kitchens,

　　finger the chemical load binding atoms.

You: a tetrapod

                    sarcopterygian

scavenger

                         hunter

gatherer

            in permanent delicto

so good at eco-niching—

    will show up and smash the ovens

            eat the cakes

Listen, therapsid (beast-face)

    Get the molecular memo : :

every heart of every species unfolds

from the self-same germs : :

                the blue whale's slow car of a heart,

                    . a pygmy shrew's

            . or bumblebee-bat's hasty motor

      going bluestreak, breakneck, lickety split, dazzles

  . the earthworm's pseudohearts are wrapped around its piehole

        . and the triple-hearted cephalopod

     pumps blue-green blood through all its chambers

*   *   *   *   *   *   *   *   *   *   *   *   *   *   *   *   *   *

the shape of your heart (if human)

is similar to a pine cone

and is about the size

of your fist

*   *   *   *   *   *   *   *

if only we could learn

how a zebrafish's broken heart regrows like a strawberry flower

just turned delectable

fruiting

over and over, press it

to your lips—

the little muscle closes up its wounds in seconds—

I'm sorry to inform you that your resting heart rate

and a cockroach's are the same

my heart's electrical output reaches out

below the line, squiggling

like a tadpole-

tail in black and shows

its shadows of hurt ("probable previous anteroseptal" attack)

but not its

affinities and loves

mother   daughter   woman   dolphin   otter   kitten

* * * * * * * * * * * * * *

also, every limb or fin budded from the same branch

every brain

anything that has a head

your inner Organizer (a patch

of tissue that tells your body

how to bend and fold)

the homeobox that told your skull

and tail where to arrange

themselves tells tales too

to a fruitfly or

what tells a cell to be

belly-side

the clear jelly cushioning

your neck bones was invented by a notochord worm!

while the zone of polarizing activity ("sonic hedgehog") makes sure your pinky

differs from your thumb

and puts a chicken's wings not where they want

but where they go

Smell that pigshit?

Smell that steak?

A hagfish or a lamprey

helped you.

*   *   *   *   *

You have a vestigial tail, a whale
has her vestigial legs

You lost how to swing from trees, the whale
how to run down the street

*   *   *   *   *

A lizard shed its limbs and took piercing toxic tines for tooth, but you
are the bigger disaster
because the babakoto lemur is indeed the father of your little boy
and you forgot it

*   *   *   *   *   *   *   *   *   *   *   *

(I don't mean to hold you here, indri, in an animal prison)

*   *   *   *   *   *   *   *   *   *   *   *

The rattler has a poison-fang

                                     yet it also has a warning

the gold in the frog's golden

                                                  dart,

the ochre fur of the velvet ant

all say "move away"

yet you, human,   give little warning of your warring

you hear a car engine hammering adrift

     on airwaves from the freeway and it's

a bee gunning its plump mini-engine

     past your ear, saying: back away

     from the sunflower! bees in their ipseity

       being only, always, themselves
will sweep equal waxy spheres along perfect planes of intersection
       or overnight

       in your cucurbit, mathematically precise before you
     even heard of hexagons or had eaten honey, having solved

       earlier than you certain mathematical figures

you love and hate the numbers, abstractions

    tethering bodies because you love

all the hard

    things

            stone bone boner beak

and yet (addendum) you love

    all the soft things too

        gastropod pussy baby boob

You, an animal of this is/was

          of what that sun was

have become a weather that hinders but are still

    a beast of wonder—pondering what sun- or

moon-

              light fell

      from skyward across your face

illuminating your beautiful mouth, now

you open it and your voice

    is bounced through space

        to your beloved lover

& deeper down,

     what you use to swallow &

              gab moves the shark's gills

     your surfaces

               can't contain the ripples

     your thinking body touching

deep & far

     in-

     divisibly   * * * * * * * * * * *

* * * * * *

you've come in

        with these pre-existing closely allied species

you've known them

& wondered, is when we made hours

how we made human? When

we coined coin

how we broke

hominin from homonym, snapped

the tail-tale buried in the back?

                    *   *   *   *   *

in fear some

      drained the animal

manuscripts of who

they named hu

      man

                    *   *   *   *   *

you are a survivor

    you, a true

        chimera, cobbled

together from bits of genetic

          trash like syntax and the poem folds out

      from all that's also unreadable in you

the synonym's in

        your DNA

like a sun some gene shines through

            the surface structures

so I can look deep

               into your irises

          as in the living eye the glad

      light glows out pluripotent then

blows out

         the spinning central disk

     past gravitational forces and

          interstellar dust

"Behold the face of nature bright

         with gladness," barely known to us beginning

          how many million years, we say, "My ago!

My love!"

Lie down here

    in the

sand

    with me

and see the

    surprise of a

seabird shadow at

    Baker Beach

moving over us

    showing our possible flight as we heat on blankets under the sun

with a bag of potato chips

if I look up the World (appears),

"the earth together with all its [parts], peoples,

    and natural features" (Google)

you move without knowing what for toward a me, & this binds you

    to cuckoos & hammock-making caterpillars

if the white butterfly knew why

    she lays her eggs on the cabbage leaf

    she might spend her hours in perplexed reflection yet

even an ant has its *petite dose de raison*, and won't

    walk straight into the fire; and you

must learn to live with yourselves and all you carry;

if you were small enough to eat your way through

    the inner layers

        of an apple leaf

            you'd see cellulose from the p.o.v.

of a microlepidopteran miner; taste it with your

                Eye

                Ear

                Hand

                Tongue

apparatuses all begun in some other kind of body   *   *   *

below you a set of strata studded

    with fossil remains does throw light

        if you dig down

    with the leaves and bones of those

        whose lines died out; yet even

the dinosaurs have their remnants—

There's one singing on a branch now!

the rocks plainly declare how extinction has acted, now

how much more would the world hold, of
you?

Polishing the Animal Mirror

Bioluminescence

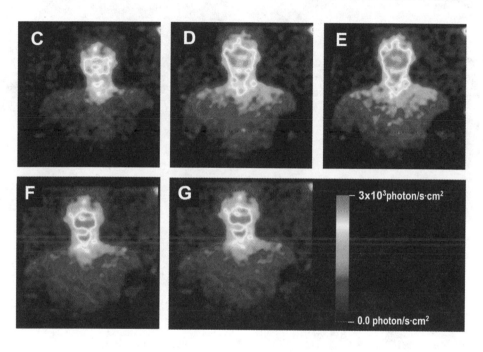

in the book called

BIOLUMINESCENCE

we all went aflame

Animal Light

some damp wood will
give off a glow

o marine vertebrates & those who go
spine-free
o fungi
    o
       firefly

come

light up the caverns & taverns
in counter-illumination camo

bacteriogenic light, your
autogenic (self-made) light, flashing libid-
    inally, luciferin, lucifer-
       ase, easy now, come down
          off that high sky

If you see by the light of dead fish & flesh
What will you read in the long night?

I will read words to bring my head back to my heart

Noctiluca   my night-light

& *if* the luminous property were
   your brain, "a
      most brilliant amethyst about
         the size" of a pin-
head, could you win

a small world not smash it ?

I once swam
in the milky whiteness of that water, crystal
train spreading with each body-
push, nighttime, Peloponnese, 1985

I was camping on the beach
with twelve transient Poles (had a crush
on a catholic boy among them), pre Cold
War border softenings

The sea was our bathtub and
   showering place, I'd stumbled there
in full-night water-alive-with-light   & ever since that liquid

phosphorus, twinned in the dark

    upper limits, I've hoped

for more glow.   I recall other

episodes: 1) a red spreading

visible hum around my bare foot in the sand, home-

   town, nighttime; and

2) a rainbowy

array around some of the most awake

     eyes I've ever

seen: underwater encounter with a

cuttlefish, Caribbean. To throw

  your glowing arm

    off & watch it twitch

on the seafloor so

your eater won't eat all of you! O yes,

  I could dangle a lighted lure

    in front of my mouth and you'd

swim in, never knowing both mouth

and barbel are me. A larval
   glowworm spins silken snares
      hanging in halos of light
  in a cave's
dark embrace. Some

humans' life dream
   is to capture a giant squid whose eye
      (the size of your head) is made to witness
the puniest prey luminesce

     in the fathomage, word
that absorbs its own light.   Imagine

     a red-tide night
  when the waters go glowy, seeing
a giant squid move
  in luciferase wakes.

We don't make our own
   bodily light but "lucifer"
we invented. The ugliest animal
on earth? How

can all that beauty we see see

    back at us. Ah,

but a snake and a tick can sense your

infrared and you do glow

at weak levels

  Your face

bathed in free radical lipids

  fluorescing rhythmically most brightly after

noon.

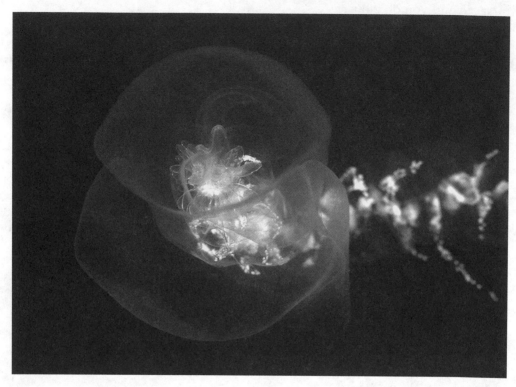

many small zooids

in conflagration / a together-flashing / a congregation is a

    flocking a gathering a talking / not talking

How Some Other Animals Do Colonies

"This larva is radially symmetrical and has no mouth."

What is an individual?

What if you were a colony?

Probably you did. You are.

All you who decided to go unitary. With infantry.

Like slicing deep through a thigh with a sharpened time packet.

All you who remained modular or all you who

say and say and say

something we think is self.

A soft whistling that never ends.

You are replying to your environment. What

has your environment asked?

thinging to make one being beyond

beyond   our ken

Ken

Bestiaries on the Lamb

Unmane

Out from deep grass
lions would
line the streets,
lie down, &
feed

themselves to dwellers

offering up
lion heart

To eat the heart of a lying
down lion

clean
coeur de lion

clown lion
lying
human
down

in a place where one grass blade makes

the next grass blade's shade

that grass blade made

the next grass blade's root

that grass blade's root

shaped it like a foot for the next

grass blade's blade that

cut it to the quick

quick wick

of lion life

flame

Frigatebird Backwards is not Agate, but Language Has us Here
(Near the Salish Sea)

an uncurable

greasy magnetism grips us

against the globe without the hemispheric sleep of frigate-

birds, who lift from earth & for many weeks won't touch down:

not water, nor rock, nor dirt; birds half-full of wakefulness. Without

motors, we cannot lift but sometimes wing our way through sleepfulness.

Friday Harbor (—where I am), in nonparallel spin to undersea mammalian

whirling. Through a kitchen window, a milk cup in a pool of light reminds us

of the child's most social mouth to which the cup will at some point be lifted, since

it's human, & has hands. Are you looking out or in? In. The child's

irrelevant/irreverent mouth, like how light sounds in a pool, or

legs swishing by one another underwater; the milk cup

spins; the harbor continues its long flight of wake

fulness, voicing a fricative industry, sounds

of sleep and sea lap lap, the hemispheric-

within that's beyond globes and grips us

to each other in mag-

netism, in-

curable.

Field, Forest, Cloth, Road

what animal running through the leaves, across the green or screen

the calf whose eyes I was gazing into

the bottom of deep brown where I had fallen

then the calf had fallen down

and I was eating it

foxes and wolves go

into the village and play with the children

Chernobyl foxes go

Fukushima crows go flying

"No one told the stork," wrote the child under her drawing

Not the crows greedy at radiocesium-soaked persimmons aflame

—strangest orange equation—at the tips of blacked-silk branches

one woman dreams she's given birth to a puppy with the head of a hedgehog

she gets lost with the lemur in the tapestry, tangled up near the surprised lion

the tarsier-lizard-monkey with one eye sleeping and one eye alert is at the heart

of the matter

The deer leaping away from the car in my dream

polishing my animal mirror

I was polishing my animal

  mirror—no

    moths appeared there

      in the single crystal genetic light

      in the dark mirror candle night

I was polishing my animal mirror, examining

    my animal teeth   a snake

        appeared in the mirror's thin

          gravel drive-

        way, someone

      had run over, had flattened it

    into permanent s-

        shape

in the animal mirror my incisors

    were not fangs but surely

    they could still tear

        meat   Yes

            the CAT   Yes the BEAR

I was polishing my animal

    mirror practicing noninvasive

    knowing and wondering

about control

     the magic kin

magic skin of this animal mirror

"Don't worry, that's just me," you say to yourself

    shining like a violet ground beetle under a stone

Sea stars are near vertebrates over to the left

    coelacanth on the far side riding toward you and birds

   Reptilian branch aflame on the plain

In the animal mirror mollusks are inching toward earthworms who

    touching themselves touch earth anew

       each time they move

*Last night, I wore a bronze broad-winged hawk foot around my neck
and a peacock feather in my ear*

I am addicted to birds

some birds are addicted to beads

satin bowerbirds have a surprised blue beadeye with which they seek bright items

and Gila monsters, which are beaded, are addicted to dreams

    of venomous lizardy things, never

dreaming of themselves as beaded purses

                            Seamless

dreamed purses purge themselves

to become beaded lizards again and

    my dreams are about birds but when birds

dream of me we cross mid-sky like

two fist- or wing-sized black holes in flight colliding

   (it's not-light self-corroding) then

      passing each other eye-by-eye—

My dream says Hi

The birds': Good-bye!

Then I dreamed of dazzling trash-eating lyrebirds who herd

   jewel-colored blazing beads   & hover

over evolution, gate-crashing   the divide

Walking Bear Creek in snOw

What is held inside the

zer O

inside the O egg (possibly my head) I heard

the rattlesnake coiled & slipped

into the brush to the side of the trail as it poised, ready

to strike & telling me

about it

then my foot rattling the dry brush, rhyming

and it's its own meme now, I'll always hear it not

laughing but being

that was its being-sound

on the path, the bugs moving the dead rabbit around

its grammar and phoneme rattling

inside the big tin can of

the world like anyone's

How do you know?

I know because I speak a language too

a lung-language night can hear

in its big empty bald head

      Other Voice (correction):

      it wasn't a rabbit, it was

      a rat or a mouse

Does it matter?

      Yes, it matters which body.

And I filmed it, the flies

      slipping in and out of a body hole

& beetles under the corpse

  eating & egg-laying &

moving the corpse around

as if the corpse would rise to life

in its being eaten

& it does

it

rises to life

my girl, my girl

Tell me something about it

who sees in sound

We came to think we
'd thought everything
then we knew we
hadn't
& we didn't
& we wouldn't
for other animals
had thought other
things & there was
no way of knowing
or thinking what
these things were

how a crab cerebrates
  a hardened harried escape
    across sands damp with night &
had a grackle recongressed its torn skin & kin
    its kind on unvertiginous grasses earthbound
all albatrosses deduced aerodynamic efficiency in adjacent air
if you tap two pebbles together can you tell
how deep the cave is if you were a bat you'd do it

in a throat-squeeze, tongue-click

staring a rock in the face & the rock

is staring you back, rocks

become you, worn

lightly, your rock-

face, gold & grey

To Do: Write Cephalopod Poem

I write something down for my future self.

I want it to change what my self does later.

I want it to make my future self know the past thought.

Rude time has a role in this.

It's been me-now and me-then all along

       in a feedback loop.

Weird—the "then" can occupy a past or a future—

   (*I was a child then*)

   (*Then when I'm a hundred I'll hoot like an owl*).

Now I'm writing, *Write cephalopod poem.*

Like a fish that sends itself a signal: *This electrical output is from me!*

   so it doesn't get confused by another fish's message, mistake

   itself for someone else.

I'll read those marks later and know what to do: *Write cephalopod poem.*

   Or who I am, writing. I am signaling

   to myself to get organized, just like cells

   tangled up in trying to build a tentacle.

Here, I've written it. *Cephalopod Poem.* Along with everything else

going on inside you, it's a memory

of the first chemical kisses

not on earth, because earth didn't exist yet

when all this kissing started.

All the Living Living Together

(Reevolutionize)

Chemical Kisses

Volcanoes

   (National Park)

Believe it or not volcanoes are keeping you

wet & warm, punching nutrients

up from the core, draping earth in shapes

you know—valley, trough, crest, mountain—volcanoes

are makers. I came to Volcanoes

to see volcanoes

        and I saw them

on this upwelling of earth's molten mantle

            having landed near Aloha Mufflers & wondered

                who on earth earth could belong to

barren at Volcanoes but elsewhere

            covered in the lush stuff dirt makes

We could tell a remarkable story

about the continents & all

that's hidden, molten & mineral,

liquid rock

hosting secretive gems & metals

) the humans

           hacking to extrude them

               intrude on the story :(

The ancients thought of wells as eyes

and said so with their words (το μάτι, in Greek;

in Phoenician it's ◁●▷ ; well + eye)

The first lexicographer of Arabic

      al-Khalīl

who made his living from falconry and gardening

wrote a dictionary, called it

"the source," and the sound

of the springs, the sound of the eye, *ayn*, he considered

the first letter, its sound from down

in the throat, at root

of us

like German spa or spew spelled backwards *weeps* or *ops* (Greek again), *eye*

but a lava eye is

what wide wilder, what deeper

) and how could this *terre* be *territory?*

"Of regions defended by animals," 1774, the *terr* of *terrify*; scaring others off a
    plot :(

) there's def. some scarring in the story :(

At night, the light reflects
    off lava gasses & flushes
        vog (volcanic smog)
as you would a smoke-bird from
    a fire-hole (65 miles down) where
        a big lava lake lies awake
    day & night
           like an illuminated coral snake
coiled dormant and blazing in the rock

        This is not a serpent you want to lightly wake

The glow spit up at dinner then
      died—I could see it
from the Volcano Restaurant—eye
    of volcano looking up from unfringed
    earth-socket singeing its
        own lashes

When a volcano blinks
    you bet the sea boils

Let's throw a politician in there!

It's not enough to tell a volcano

    she's wonderful, you better go

        for stupendous, the best

            of her kind You can see why

the *'ōhi'a* flowers are red-

      fringed, as if bit

           at the lip on their way out the earth

The ranger tells me

her fat dog once fell

into a lava tube & was lost there

for two days till her skinny dog

shewed her the way:

beneath some fern fronds, two

blue eyes looking up

from the dark

as if bodies could be swallowed

    back to earth but

        live to

bark the tale, which might have several endings:

fat dog ever after got less food

so she could get out if trapped again

or

fat dog ever after got more food

since you only live once

a splinter of fire eye

an unopened rock

above which a body

   stars,

       opens out,

      splinters,

      and stars

rain shadow or mountain

shadow, like word

shadow—what it

   casts

     out of itself in

darkness or hides

there, on the other side

   (of sky)

I shelter in word shadow when possible

   (*shew* an old shadow of *show*)

and dreamt a

distant glow of the gold

red heart behind the

mountains (a poem laid out

on white hills) something was

cooking & shewing its heat

through the page I think

it's the lyric simmering

beneath the folds

) human & humanless

) history & historyless

where what light stars listen to

muddles, shines

and finite lava

   bodies forth, venting

   from what seemed soundless, immovable rock

that's the thing, when

I saw (I can't claim I

"looked into") the lava hole what

I was actually seeing I can't
   say—an opening, a scar
   a busted pore from which
the depths of earth
       give face
because
17 major plates float
on a softer, bitter, hotter, buttery
chamber

later, I swim at a black sand beach
made from lava, green
sea turtles napping

bright orange butterflies snapped
into air, detonations of time & flame

mongoose (brought to eat black rats, the rats brought on ships) sneaking out
towards trash under coconut trees
It turns out, rats are nocturnal
mongooses diurnal
nene goose and other native bird eggs on the menu, not rats

peach-headed finch & his less
sunsetish partner

for example, freaking out

over bread crumbs from

lotso vacationing Americans in bathing suits, none of them flame-colored,
    none of them gold

when I want gold

I want it like a feeling once hosted in rock that simmers now in the throat

something you can't eat:

red-headed bird with white throat-band, black body

a yellow-billed cardinal

which is actually a tanager, native

to Brazil and Argentina

yesterday, a kalij pheasant rustled out of the bushes in the national park, it

came from the Himalayan foothills and here

fucks up the plants

some bird's been eating berries, I can see

by the windshield/shitshield

maybe a mynah brought from South Asia

to eat army worms, it came like me & other invaders

trash-eating and full of voice

It's a fistfight:

here

     vs

    there

rock

      vs

    flight

and the sound of the bird

which might caw, which might sing

and the fire

melts rock and intermediaries it for us

so I can say

like a lava bird this poem squawks & hums

toward a sea stack housing the last Kanaloa plant

though it is not in my purview to name the great goddess who made this place

you can see her hair and tears if you look

sometime back

   with the gods you fly

away from that island

of your birth

) earth—that

                      island in the sky (:

you fly home

you twist yourself again around winter's

white bone in the old country

   (which old country?)

around as against

your spine vagrant, variant, against its ossuary

like a bird or lava flow, a word migrates

you have to wonder

what were volcanoes before they were volcanoes

a burning mountain, Vulcan's forge, Etna being the first

to be so-called

what was anything called before

it was called home

   called home

volcanoes don't echo such endings

what comes out of one

we try to make our own

'alalā crows

   caw

a red ribbon of visible sound

but lost a note that humans

    stole

I once read poems under the eye of a volcano

which was something akin to talking towards earth's heart

    and feeling heard

the space between words is inside you, lava-like

each word bright cellular packet of living

    energy

how the word and world hold in their own toward breaking

    free

will heart

will heart heart
and hard harden

will will will it
  or aggregate
      around a grain again

after any rude stress
      a tree will alter its bark and dress
    like land after lava flow

to imagine to mars with moon as your lantern
to study cracked stars
to travel with ghosts & let go o
        heartwill

break back soft
  as an oyster, sharp
  as its shell slicing
what forthcoming flesh
      stores for or in us

The Promises of Air

and I who am cold

that

world-cold

of mechanical go(l)d when

words

because they are attached

to nothing, *gratis*, go

floating through air where

live, yes, birds

warming the sound of that rhyming empire

pulling words out of the everyday world by snapping the neck of meter

for the road ahead

which will be air, for sure

    ≥

each word there

mad fair

delinked and flying

I heard the saw of feathers first, then

3 black forms whuffing

from the left, cuffing right

Crows, compass of their whuff and world,

sounded like a flock of small women

clearing their throats before diving into a pool

2 chasing the other, noisy

wings & cawing

So *what was the crow story?*

Two parents crazy to encourage a fledgling?

A thief? an interloper? why so pissed off?

A corvid ménage gone to the minus?

From the ground, no way to know

Here where the words lick the human forms with their dirt-driven skins

But there is the instant after the woman leaves the ground, before

her head hits the water

stars have replaced circles in affinities among crows

Once Water's Heart—The hand The land

If you were a child
standing on the grass holding an ice cube in your hand
   and your hand was warm, was warming
or if you were the earth holding an iceberg in your belly
        the bathing veins feeding the heart

And if the ice, the mountains were talking
      to the animals walking over them
The mountains and the clouds
encouraging them
     The foxes and The bears
or scolding them
     The rabbits and The deer

The hand, the land heating

Yes, I care about icebergs
more than I care about you, she said   No,
no, I don't
care about icebergs
more than I care about you, she
said, I do
I do

The ice embroidering the animals

      stitching them in   hoof and

                                  tuft

The animals embroidering the ice   step by   step

If the child held out her hand

and the wolves walked over it

The friction between paw and palm igniting

The one cooling the one heating the other

And if the child's hand

Was too hot now

To hold anything

Crystalline heart melting in our hands

Flame could not destroy these mountains

because they were made outside the mind

and animals are etched there

also in the blood in your hand

Husband Heart Dream

I ate my dead husband's heart

size of a chicken heart

large for a chicken, small for a man

removing the thin lenticular of glass

from the back

of the heart where it

accrues—heart's

filter, like a fine

glass film

or

glass stone such

as you would find as

a nugget of lint in a vacuum catch, lodged

at heartback

the word *quoit* ("curling stone," 1388) could describe it

then

I ate his heart

to keep faith, to keep strong

if

your glass palate comes loose
"Take that out of your mouth!" says mother
your glass mouth-trap asunder and crumbling in
saltlike shards in the night on your dry, dreaming
tongue for "jihadists" or "viruses" to forage and hoard

                  cover the body with
        a white cloth as
one does to
distinguish the dead
from the living
Because
the face of death
has a glass heart to it, it
synonyms forward in the mouth toward
what in the world we
can't spit out, but like the world we have
already eaten
what I love.

Deevolutionize

Picture of, not a

This is not a picture of a bird.

It is not of a hoop, a
     hula, nor
     Saturn's fiery, fading rings.

It is not a picture of
     the sun around which our
     planet spins, or the sky
     or ethers in which
     they do it.

This is not a picture of
     a mobster, a monster
     nor a god.

Not a picture of the gorgeous
     teal-loving sea in which
     your pappou bathed.

Because sometimes we name things for things
they are not, and this is not a picture of

Hydra

the wettest island on my tongue

should be trembling

with ropy, snaking streams

is dry underfoot.

Not a picture of any water at all.

Nor TV antennas on hilltops or buildings, not

military ships with cannons pointing toward shore, not trees,

not leaves.

Just as a dog is not a dog

    even to other dogs

and a bird is not a bird

    even to itself

if we have forgotten how

we are fathers or mothers, sisters, daughters, children, brothers,

you remember

when you hear a baby cry

how the *f* of feather floats

in aether but if the *f* of father sinks in water

we lose its fame, its name, its errant aim

which was once a way

of condensing thought or light or shade.

If you cannot make a picture of hunger, you cannot make a picture of a word.

Sparta through a Hole in the Past (Correspondences)

I hoot like an owl on the roof

I am an ordinary girl

even your iPhone can't capture it

because I'm from Sparta

where leaves late night look

    cut from bald trees

Circling the dusty internet café off the main drag

in a white rental car

with holes in the floor I can see

the asphalt blurring through all the way back to

Sparta, I've invented a harvest

of words, bright bitcoin, you can see

straight through the years shot through with air

back to me

harvest	-	you
bright	-	I
late	-	I
leaf	-	you
bitcoin	-	they
night	-	us

owl   -   it

asphalt   -   it

floors   -   we

see   -   you

air   -   us

years   -   i / I

rip the body

stitch it back

rip the body

take out the years/dirt

pigskin

pokémon

samsung

if *you* doesn't have a capital neither does *it*

rip the Apple

out of the body-

branch   strip

it   ringed

body working

the dirt   rip

the ipod off

       stitch it

back up   rip

bitcoin out

of the body sack   stitch it

back up   slackening   rip the

stitch it

Starbuck

pigskin stitch it

mute

body

rip

Sparta off your face

strip your

history dress

in a   space between the dash and the word

          the most volcanically active

word

in our solar system

is

it's so easy to say

You

You do

    your *thing*   you

do you

    thou, not

    thing   you, pro-

(so flexy) noun—first

you're *self-talking*, soon you're *pointing*, next you're *gathering* with it, moving

one people around. Come, people! You   *a hem*

    eow (Old English)   *yus* (Proto-Indo)

  a hummingbird-little word   *thieving*

heaving   against the palate with so much heft

(when I say *you* I make a little trough with my tongue)

  are you holding   history at all

             :

    I'm waiting for trains with children & friends

        amen

I is the binding herein

  you is the glue

Delicately positioned mirrors track the squeezing and stretching
of space as gravitational waves go by

Two black holes slid toward each other making
   a pig's big
      nostril holes in the sky
One big snout
     sniffing out space

Did you hear the rattling antennas?
My question is
   is it rhythmic?

Time wrapped around you in a
   snug dark glove and you
      fell loving out of light like—you fell
   out of light or light
rushed out of you

When a mass 31
   times the sun
and one 25x collide
   they create a smash-hole of 53 solar masses

—I'd say you're missing some.

If three = thee,

    that is what you hear now hissing, not the fridge's home

      hum, not the sound

  of money gushing but the chirp of

     ancient space

like gossip-sound going sideways

     across dark, lake-ish skies

(what gossip did space make?) Does it rhyme?

      = The breathing in of all living. The

                 exhalation of the dead. =

At the uncrisp edge, space

  twists, divides, and time

    trembles, scrambles

  and leaks like weather

Did you tear yourself out

  of the visible universe?

Yes, one day I did.

Laser Interferometer Gravitational-Wave Observatory (LIGO),
Simulating eXtreme Spacetimes (sxs project), simulation of two black holes colliding

I had some k/t/re/e/ys

      (after Joy Harjo)

I had some keys that looked

into locked doors in books & trees.

Open the lake: a book.

Open the book: a lake.

Some trees, some keys, they

would frame & name each other

all day, coughing and knocking in crevices.

I had some keys that didn't open anything at all

or that peeled back their bark & stood

trembling, tumbling one

from the other   *k* shaking itself from *t*

Some trees were feeling vulnerable, naked

I left a note for my key, my tree

      folded it, tucked it

      into the heartwood

Paper note,

torn from the tree's key body

folded back at heart:

to disenthrall my mind from machines twig by twig, twine by twine

to make the tree song long

er

In the Theater of the In/Compatible

(All of the Living Living Together)

Your body would so

laugh that into earth

your body would laugh that

    into the earth

      ***

it was made by breathers

      ***

some of the breathers were beetles

and some of the breathers were worms

some of the living you breathed was exhaled from sponges

and some of that living from mosses

some of the breathers are grasses

and some of their number are birds

some of the breathers bacteria

some absolutely loud babies

all of their number have kin

***

laugh that into the earth

laugh that into the air

the phytoplankton making oxygen there

***

Once time began to exist, it was impossible for it to end on its own, one of your
number wrote down

The true performance is the animals on earth, another of that number uttered

***

we would add trees

we would add rocks

we would add water

***

in the persistent smell of identity

hanging like a glistening messy cloud

around your body   you laughed it

into the earth

no better house

   or bark

no better word

   or thighs

no better butter

   or mind

no better poem

   or life

no better anther

   or world

     ***

wet flower,

   (you were) born

la joie se produit par une petite compréhension entre cause et effet

S

un battement d'ailes ?

Sfakiá to Loutró

In the morning the goats were saying hey hey hey
from the maquis and later, in the evening,
they were saying ha ha ha

from the boat, the raw cliffs of southwest crete
and a little tiny cloud like a thin handkerchief, worn
to diaphaneity, clinging to the black
jaw of a cave

what turquoise lapping & ribboned like
a band along a girl's hair
like no time

the girl is now or the girl is ancient and therefore dead but
remembered in stone or clay

just as she was born into a history
she didn't make
and then continued making it

she died in time

and out of it

and minnows like apostrophes, asphodels hanging, darting

in the clear water

more or less november

First it was five when it used to be six, and we had more light in the morning.

Then it was four when it used to be five, and it was darkening and damp. It was

two when it used to be three, and twelve when it used to be one, and we wondered

where such a ghostly packet could go   skidding or slipping

        —through holes in air?   Who

had whittled their canines down or dropped

the slinking vertebrae for branches, who

no longer

boned

at the hip   How

hours accumulate in the bowl

of the pelvis, 3 million

years balanced

in bipedal performance, the ring

of bone the baby

squeezed through

each invisible hour sliding in air   How they stick

to the sacrum! ilia & ischia   a flaring   unfolding

                           ossified

                                  lily,   rough

      juncture

we keep trying to define: when the hip

tilted and said a torso

went perpendicular to the sky not

parallel to the ground except in sleep

is that sky a huge feeling

in the back of your mind, skull

reaching up to kiss it

I'm never going back, you thought, so

wanting to be *humaigne*

(of earth), *(dh)ghomon* (human), not as opposed

to gods, who live in air but the other

fleshy things,   & the plants

Gravity made time go but the further we pulled from ground

where minutes should have more drag

our tails

dropped and we could no longer move

Through trees

With ease

With casc

         Be

more Liquid

more Light

Αστυνομία Νοσοκομείο

I keep confusing words, calling

policemen hospitals,

mayors townhalls.

I mistook Corinthian Power Plant

for an ancient palace,

   deep harbor

for dream. Then I remembered language

is a lingering we keep hoping will draw

up exigence like water

   from a well, metal

dust toward magnetite. Like this: in Lefkada, the old woman told me a story

as we walked by her village's tongued

   harbor. In winter the waves sometimes

      lap right up into the streets, and when she was a child a child

   was taken that way while his sister played and the mother

was out working the fields. When the mother came home the daughter said

Don't bother looking for Kosma, a wave

   ate him. How astounding then the accuracy

of language and wave.

                        Sometimes it licks clean, licks

the pot clean.

allow us what's hidden

should your clean body curve
round the blue keel
of ice shadowing below water
you would know

the slice between light and depth when
all light is bound

should you shout
no sound

but at the surface
ice grains scatter light bits and bounce them
toward your scattering mind

what do you love here?

you wanted to say "this crystal"
"this curve and cloud of you"
but there is no you here

this ice is free of what you know

Glossary

Cephalopod: You probably know these beloved friends (octopuses, etc.) are mollusks, more closely related to slugs than to us. One of the wonders is how, along a completely different evolutionary line, they developed a nervous system complex enough to trick and tease us, escape our tanks, steal our cameras, and dismantle toy submarines. They "think" through the length of their tentacles. With life spans of one to three years, they gather all this knowledge on the run.

Glass figure, Rudolf and Leopold Blaschka, Argonauta argo (c. 1860–90)

Corncrake: bird in the rail family, whose call sounds a lot like a busted, crackling electrical wire. Discussing how animals change habitats before adapting bodily to the new landscape, Darwin writes, "Hence it will cause [. . .] no surprise . . . that there should be long-toed corncrakes living in meadows instead of in swamps; that there should be woodpeckers where not a tree grows . . ." (186, *Origin*).

Cucurbit: plant in the gourd family, including melons, squashes, and cucumbers. Ground bees sometimes overnight in their flowers. I have found them there trysting in my garden. It can also mean a small container, like an alembic. Ghost-memory of a genie in a cucurbit from *One Thousand and One Nights*, though I've never found it again.

Eusthenopteron: an extinct lobe-finned fish; *eustheno*—strong, *pteron*—wing; strong-winged, strong-finned. Those powerful fins were like primitive legs allowing eusthenopteron to move through mud from water hole to water hole as oceans dried up.

Exapt: making good use of tools invented for other purposes; example: feathers were originally developed for warmth but later allowed former reptiles to fly.

Fenestra: a small natural hole or opening, esp. in a bone. Your middle ear is connected to your inner ear by this tiny window.

Gerygone: bird "born of sound"; peep-warblers.

Homeobox: the DNA sequence responsible for putting our bodies together in the proper shape. By "our" I mean animals, fungi, plants, many other eukaryotes. This little string is involved in transcription of the manuscript, like ancient scribes copying out Sappho's poems in the (in)correct order.

Hybridogenesis: This is wild and lovely, from Donald I. Williamson, via Lynn Margulis. Williamson writes, "My idea is that metamorphosis [e.g., caterpillar to butterfly] represents an evolutionary legacy: A change in genetic expression during development from one taxon to another, and it is testable." Search for his name + "hybridogenesis" + "onychophorans." It is not proved, and maybe even a little crazy, but let it complicate our metaphors.

Indri: a lemur with lichen-colored eyes, also called babakoto ("little father" or "ancestor" in Malagasy). In captivity, it does not live longer than a year or reproduce. Sings in chorus each morning. To hear them, look up "indri chorus" + "Andasibe, Madagascar." (Critically endangered.)

Kingdom: Of uncertain origin; I choose the roots that go through "kin," and lead away from "doom." No king in this kingdom. You take the Queen, says the orchid; I'll take the Ace, says the bee. How many Kingdoms of Life you count depends on when and where you live (most phylogenists currently say somewhere between five and eight). We've used these systems to classify relations between all living things, which means they're rife with hierarchy. (In which kingdom do viruses belong?) A kingdom is a conceptual space. Poetry is a form of deep phylogeny that turns the kingdom round. Life won't be classified, even when we dwell in the kingdoms of the dead.

Labyrinthodont:

 an early amphibian precursor, ancestor to everything that has a spine and lives on land. Did they invent the skull? Their teeth, crosscut, contained labyrinths, and you come to think there is no myth we invented that other animals did not also invent but not with human sounds.

Nucleotide: building material for DNA and RNA in every living thing. (Viruses hack nucleotide sequences to replicate.) Have always loved the mysterious wash of this word.

Opsin: conjugated protein in your eye that catches photons, allowing sight. Many mushrooms also have them, not to mention jellyfish, fruit flies, bacteria, and algae.

Paleomaps: configurations of ancient oceans and land before we lived here. You probably know that Colorado was once covered in shallow seas. Maybe you know that the landmasses Laurasia (now Europe, Asia, and North America) and Gondwana (Africa, South America, Antarctica, Australia, and India) smashed into each other, making the Appalachians and other things. To be noted: we're still in motion.

Patagium: fold of skin between a fore- and hind-limb.

Petite dose de raison: a little dose of reason—even ants have it; from Swiss entomologist Pierre Huber, referenced in *Origin* in relation to instinct.

Phototrophic: light-eating, like plants, and some bacteria. I have never stopped being amazed that plants make their own food, inside their own bodies.

Piehole: That's your mouth.

Preauricular sinus: Called a "malformation," it's a small benign hole where the rim of the human ear meets the face, an early ancestor trace.

Prokaryote: "before the nut" of the nucleus; no nesting bag for DNA—it all floats freely in one sack. Many eat at the same table with you, for example, in your gut. You, of course, are a eukaryotic assemblage of cells that store cakes of DNA in a little citadel inside each cell, a sign of early prokaryotic mergers across kingdoms.

Samara:

a fruit with a wing to travel by, aka whirligig, wingnut, spinning jenny; many trees have them, including maples, ash, and elms

Sarcopterygii: the lobe-finned fishes from which tetrapods arose.

Silurian: a geologic period ending about 419 MYA (million years ago), in which it seems the first multicelled species tried life on land (club mosses and ferns and the first relatives of centipedes and spiders). All kinds of things happened then to make the later explosion of land-life possible, including weather that steadied itself.

Sonic hedgehog: is a signaling protein (made from genetic code and named for a video game character) that orchestrates certain body patterns, like brains, fingers, and toes. I gather all this information and wonder: what were all the animal experiments that allowed this information to be carried to me?

Synapsid: a reptile of the Permian and Triassic that began to invent the mammal.

Tetrapod: four-footed (four-limbed) animal. Birds are tetrapods (two of their feet are wings), whales are (their forelimbs are flippers, but the legs have melted into time), and so are we. Some, like snakes, lost all four limbs and we wonder where and how and why.

Therapsid: the ancestors that moved said limbs more directly under the body (rather than sprawling like a lizard's). Though the first ones were reptilian, mammals are the only living therapsid remnant. *Ther*—beast, *apsid*—arch (of the skull). Beast-head, beast-face. You.

Tiktaalik: another transitional figure in the movement from fish to land-walker. Probably the first creature to have a neck(!), which allows for stealthier predation on land, I guess.

Umbel:

many tiny flowers held umbrella-like

Zygoma: a diamond-shaped bone stretching from below the eye socket to the eye-side; from the Greek for "yoke" or crossbar (how oxen were hitched to the plow); helps protect your neural-processing systems; by you I mean humans, birds, reptiles, mammals, and ancestral but not living amphibians. If you press your fingers to your cheekbones under your eyes and gently palpate toward your temples, you'll feel the yawn of the ⌒ heading toward your skull.

A Few More Notes

Reading these poems you might ask: Where are the mushrooms? Where are the bacteria? The all-important viruses? Why so zoocentric? What are chromista? (Kelp, mildew, diatoms . . .) They are all around and in us in inter-kingdom entanglement, but here I am dwelling on our animal siblings.

"All life loved itself—," Fanny Howe.

Some of you who read this book may know that my daughter is an adolescent (at the time of publication, anyway) and at the opening, wonder, shouldn't teens know mothers can't write and drive at the same time? For the evolutionary record: Eva was ≈ 8 when I took this note, her friend Maggie ≈ 6.

To hear the LIGO chirp, tap "sound of two black holes colliding" into your search bar.

"In the beginning there was no doom" is from Carla Harryman's *Memory Play*.

Eléni Vakaló quote is from "Description of the Body," Karen Emmerich's translation.

"In the Great Hall of Bones": I thought "and in the night you hear the bear . . ." was inspired by Michael Donhauser in Rosmarie Waldrop's translation, but maybe it's Paol Keineg translated by Laura Marris.

To hear hibernating bear sounds, it's as easy as tapping just that into the search bar.

The word *overblooming* comes from a conversation with Dawn Lundy Martin.

Bee orchids (*Ophrys apifera*), ranging from Iran to Ireland, are flowers who dress themselves as female bees, luring males to try to mate and, in the act, pollinate the flower. Orchid bees (euglossini) are bees who visit orchids as well as "tree wounds, fungi and certain flowers," according to the U.S. Forest Service. They also seem to make perfume. Some orchids disguise themselves as enemies, and the fight is what pollinates; many have exclusive relationships with their pollinators.

"Your Kingdom" contains quotes from a number of sources, beginning with *On the Origin of Species*. Others in the poem: "I am listening to the salt inside your hunger," "ether on silk," and "you come out of dangerous plesiosaurs" are from Will Alexander, who taught me the word *exapt*. "[F]amily is a pond to you" and "cartilaginous silence" are from Henry Psanek. Ted Hughes's translations of *Metamorphoses* and Dante's *Purgatorio* are in here too, maybe in Anthony Esolen's translation. The sentence "There's one singing on a branch now!" regarding birds as dinosaur remnants was uttered by poet Reed Bye during dinner.

I have written elsewhere about the SS *Makambo*, a ship carrying fruit and copra that hit a rock near what is called Lord Howe Island in the Tasman Sea in 1918. Rats swam ashore, and soon at least six bird species, thirteen endemic insects, and a plant had been wiped out, among them the "Lord Howe" gerygone.

Another story that has haunted me, one that also appears in *Make Yourself Happy*, is the native Hawaiian ʻalalā crows losing some territorial calls and warnings because they now only live in captivity and no longer face predators. An attempt to re-release ʻalalās in 2016 did not go well, in part because of predation by ʻio hawks (until recently also listed as endangered). But the crows, including one named Kiaʻikūmokuhāliʻi, used long-distance alarm calls frequently in the three years they were in the wild. (They are apparently the loudest birds in the forest.) I do wonder if the calls are the same, or if Kiaʻikūmokuhāliʻi and his kin invented new ones. There are, as of this writing, over 110 ʻalalās living in captivity, and conservationists are working on a new re-release plan. My gratitude to the researchers at the ʻAlalā Project for helping me understand some of the call complexities. To hear some of their expressive communiqués (one sounds like a baby tiger that's had its tail gently bitten, another like a teen who just saw someone streaking across the gym in 1979), try: "ʻalalā basics" + "listen to ʻalalā calls."

"Animal Light": luciferin, luciferase: the substrate and enzyme that create a bioluminescent glow, from "lucifer," that is, "light-bringer"; was first used by Raphaël Dubois, pharmacologist from Le Mans who worked on both bioluminescence and anesthesiology.

"No one told the stork" is from Svetlana Alexievich's *Voices from Chernobyl*, translated by Keith Gessen.

"Animal Mirror" includes language from evolutionary biologist W. D. Hamilton's burial instructions and Christopher Dewdney's *Spring Trances in the Control Emerald Night: Book One of a Natural History of Southwestern Ontario*.

"Once time began to exist, it was impossible for it to end on its own" is from Yōko Tawada's *Memoirs of a Polar Bear*. "The true performance is the animals on earth," Cecilia Vicuña, in conversation.

"I had some k/t/re/e/ys," after Joy Harjo, was written during a workshop organized by Jen Foerster, Layli Long Soldier, and me. Beloved dg okpik was also present. Jen led this exercise.

"Painted cakes cannot satisfy hunger" (see Dōgen, via Gary Snyder, *Mountains and Rivers Without End*).

Many texts were important to these poems, including *The Annotated Origin: A Facsimile of the First Edition of On the Origin of Species*, James T. Costa; *Your Inner Fish*, Neil

Shubin; *Staying with the Trouble*, Donna Haraway; "What Is It Like to Be a Bat?," Thomas Nagel; many things by Lynn Margulis, always; *Other Minds: The Octopus, the Sea, and the Deep Origins of Consciousness*, Peter Godfrey-Smith; *Integrated Principles of Zoology*, seventh edition (again and again); *A Sea of Glass: Searching for the Blaschkas' Fragile Legacy in an Ocean at Risk*, Drew Harvell; *Trees of Life: A Visual History of Evolution*, Theodore Pietsch; and *Becoming Human*, Zakiyyah Iman Jackson.

Thank you to many online sources, such as Nature.com, Lexico.com, the Online Etymology Dictionary, the *New York Times*, Caltech's LIGO lab site, Biocyclopedia .com, Wikipedia, and more.

pinnipeds' flippers show a five-fingered terrestrial lineage

    common to your own yet

even without hands they are better fishers

Images and Credits

Page 3: Ernst Haeckel: phaeodaria (public domain, via Wikimedia Commons), radiolaria, lichen.

Page 5 and throughout the back matter: Tree image from Tree of Life web project.

Page 9: circular phylogenetic tree, from "Inferring the Mammal Tree: Species-Level Sets of Phylogenies for Questions in Ecology, Evolution, and Conservation." Illustration shows "relationships and tempo of diversification across mammals" in "node-dated molecular phylogeny of 5,911 extant and recently extinct species."

Page 12: "I think," from Darwin's Red Notebook "B," 1837, kept just after the voyage of the *Beagle*; his first known drawing of an evolutionary tree.

Page 25, set by HR Hegnauer: Poem-drawing by the author.

Page 32: Paleontological chart, Edward Hitchcock, 1840; the first "paleontological-based tree of life," based on a two-kingdom model.

Image throughout "Your Kingdom": circular time tree showing evolutionary timeline and relationships of 9,993 species of bird.

Page 89: "Imaging of Ultraweak Spontaneous Photon Emission from Human Body Displaying Diurnal Rhythm" by Masaki, Kobayashi et al., *DIOS ONE* 4(7), 2009.

Page 96: Giant *Praya* siphonophore (which can grow up to 130 feet long). Photo taken by diver Merry B. Fortune, permission generously granted. Further on is my attempt to draw (then collage) a hula skirt species. These animals are wild congregations of small cnidarian zooids.

Page 98: Siphonophore poem-drawing-collage by the author.

Page 99: Tapestry up close, but which tapestry?

Page 115: Herculaneum papyrus fragment 0009, Scriptor Graecus incertus, from the library carbonized by Mt. Vesuvius, Il Catalogo dei Papiri Ercolanesi online.

Page 129: Crow wings.

Page 130: Simple collage using "Familie Raben," 1854, by Johann Jakob Kaup. "Stars have replaced circles in this quinarian view of affinities among crows . . . Empty triangles stand for groups not yet discovered," writes Pietsch in *Trees of Life*.

Page 135: Maria Sibylla Merian: swallow tailed butterfly and passion flower (public domain, via Wikimedia Commons). Merian (1647–1717), artist, naturalist, botanist, entomologist, mother, was one of the first (the first?) Europeans to document evidence of insect metamorphosis, as well as to illustrate not just the animals but the foods they ate and their habitats. Pre-Linnaean systems, she was not interested in classification, "only in the formation, propagation, and metamorphosis of creatures . . . and the nature of their diet."

Page 145: Two black holes colliding, as imagined by the Simulating eXtreme Spacetimes (sxs) project.

Page 158: *Gaia Hand* by Dorion Sagan, with his permission generously granted.

Page 159: *Argonauta argo, Blaschka Nr. 549* (1885), by Rudolf and Leopold Blaschka, CMoG L.17.3.63-23. Lent by Cornell University; image licensed by The Corning Museum of Glass under CC BY 4.0. A Blaschka glass model of *Argonauta argo*, also known as the paper nautilus, held in the Corning Museum of Glass. In the days before widespread aquaria, before specimens could easily be shipped to places of study, the Bohemian father-and-son team Leopold and Rudolf Blaschka made over ten thousand scientifically accurate, beautiful glass models of seven hundred marine species, which were sent all over the world instead of dead or soon-to-be-dead animals. They also made exquisite plants and flowers, some of which can be seen at the Harvard Museum of Natural History.

Page 160: Crosscut labyrinthodont tooth illustration from *On the Genesis of Species* by St. George Mivart (1827–1900), originally published in London by Macmillan and Co., 1871.

Page 161: Samara image, drawn and generously provided by Bobbi Angell, created for the New York Botanical Garden's *Guide to the Vascular Plants of Central French Guiana*.

Page 162: Umbel illustration from *Encyclopedia Britannica*, eleventh edition.

Poems in this manuscript have been published in a number of print and online journals and anthologies, and I am very grateful to the editors of these, with shout-outs where possible:

Three Fold (Chris Tysh); *Bomb* (Chantal McStay); *Boston Review*, "What Nature" issue (Linda Russo); *Conjunctions* (Brad Morrow); *Counter-Desecration: A Glossary for Writing within the Anthropocene*, Wesleyan University Press (coedited by Marthe Reed, ever transforming in the ark hive, and Linda Russo); *Granta*; *Gulf Coast* (Emelie Griffin); *Harriet* (Michael Slosek); *Interim* (Ronaldo Wilson); *Kenyon Review* (Solmaz Sharif); *Midst* (Annelyse Gelman—check out her cool project at www.midst.press); Poem-a-Day (+ podcast version); the Poetry Project (Andrea Abi-Karam).

Two poems were commissioned by the Benaki Museum in Athens for the Fokion Zissiadis exhibit *ICEBERGS: From Genesis to Extinction*. Part of "Your Kingdom" was included in the De Appel Curatorial Programme reader for the show "Super Feelings," Amsterdam, curated by Melissa Appleton, Monika Georgieva, Ka-Tjun Hau and Chala Itai Westerman, 2022. Composer Frank Carlberg set the first section of "Your Kingdom" to music, forthcoming sometime, somewhere.

Gratitude

Laird Hunt, my closest, beloved reader, ever patient, ever present: thank you, x life times. Thanks to the Djerassi residency, where "Your Kingdom" began in 2015 (though some of the other poems here predate that), and to Yaddo, Ucross, and the Helen Riaboff Whiteley Center at the Friday Harbor Labs, where the work continued. Gratitude also to the NEA, for a generous poetry fellowship that supported some of the research and writing of this book. To Erika Stevens, who has been a terrific editor. To HR Hegnauer for saving the design day. And to Chris Fischbach, who supported my work longtime.

To Marian Drew, and her generosity in allowing use of this cover photograph from her Australiana Still Life series, done with care and respect (to animals gathered from roadkill).

Thanks to Julie Carr, Brenda Coultas, Mónica de la Torre, Marcella Durand, Forrest Gander, Imani Jackson, Cole Swensen, Anne Waldman, many others, for conversation. And to my beautiful community of poets, artists, writers, friends, and all my animal ancestors, who inspire me.

How do we read the animal when the only history is a human archive

One thing I know

the animal makes us

as we make the animal and

a piece of your past

hurts   when you fall on your ass

where you lost your tail

Coffee House Press began as a small letterpress operation in 1972 and has grown into an internationally renowned nonprofit publisher of literary fiction, essay, poetry, and other work that doesn't fit neatly into genre categories.

Coffee House is both a publisher and an arts organization. Through our *Books in Action* program and publications, we've become interdisciplinary collaborators and incubators for new work and audience experiences. Our vision for the future is one where a publisher is a catalyst and connector.

LITERATURE
is not the same thing as
PUBLISHING

Funder Acknowledgments

Coffee House Press is an internationally renowned independent book publisher and arts nonprofit based in Minneapolis, MN; through its literary publications and *Books in Action* program, Coffee House acts as a catalyst and connector—between authors and readers, ideas and resources, creativity and community, inspiration and action.

Coffee House Press books are made possible through the generous support of grants and donations from corporations, state and federal grant programs, family foundations, and the many individuals who believe in the transformational power of literature. This activity is made possible by the voters of Minnesota through a Minnesota State Arts Board Operating Support grant, thanks to the legislative appropriation from the Arts and Cultural Heritage Fund. Coffee House also receives major operating support from the Amazon Literary Partnership, Jerome Foundation, Literary Arts Emergency Fund, McKnight Foundation, and the National Endowment for the Arts (NEA). To find out more about how NEA grants impact individuals and communities, visit www.arts.gov.

Coffee House Press receives additional support from Bookmobile; Dorsey & Whitney LLP; Elmer L. & Eleanor J. Andersen Foundation; the Matching Grant Program Fund of the Minneapolis Foundation; Mr. Pancks' Fund in memory of Graham Kimpton; the Schwab Charitable Fund; and the U.S. Bank Foundation.

The Publisher's Circle of Coffee House Press

Publisher's Circle members make significant contributions to Coffee House Press's annual giving campaign. Understanding that a strong financial base is necessary for the press to meet the challenges and opportunities that arise each year, this group plays a crucial part in the success of Coffee House's mission.

Recent Publisher's Circle members include many anonymous donors, Patricia A. Beithon, Anitra Budd, Andrew Brantingham, Dave & Kelli Cloutier, Mary Ebert & Paul Stembler, Jocelyn Hale & Glenn Miller, the Rehael Fund-Roger Hale/Nor Hall of the Minneapolis Foundation, Randy Hartten & Ron Lotz, Dylan Hicks & Nina Hale, William Hardacker, Kenneth & Susan Kahn, Stephen & Isabel Keating, the Kenneth Koch Literary Estate, Cinda Kornblum, Jennifer Kwon Dobbs & Stefan Liess, the Lenfestey Family Foundation, Sarah Lutman & Rob Rudolph, the Carol & Aaron Mack Charitable Fund of the Minneapolis Foundation, Gillian McCain, Malcolm S. McDermid & Katie Windle, Mary & Malcolm McDermid, Daniel N. Smith III & Maureen Millea Smith, Enrique & Jennifer Olivarez, Robin Preble, Nan G. Swid, Grant Wood, and Margaret Wurtele.

For more information about the Publisher's Circle and other ways to support Coffee House Press books, authors, and activities, please visit www.coffeehousepress.org/pages/donate or contact us at info@coffeehousepress.org.

ELENI SIKELIANOS was born and grew up in California and has lived in New York, Paris, Athens (Greece), Colorado, and now, Providence. She is the author of nine previous books of poetry, most recently *What I Knew* and *Make Yourself Happy,* and two hybrid memoir-verse-image-novels, *The Book of Jon* and *You Animal Machine.* A number of her books have appeared in French and two in Greek, and her work has been translated into many other languages. She has been at the forefront of ecopoetics, documentary, and hybrid works since the early 2000s, exploring family as well as animal lineages. Her work has been widely fêted and anthologized, earning awards from the National Endowment for the Arts, the Fulbright Program, the National Poetry Series, the New York Foundation for the Arts, Bogliasco, Ucross, and the Gertrude Stein Awards in Innovative American Poetry, among others. Dedicated to the many ways poetry manifests in communities, she has taught workshops in public schools, homeless shelters, and prisons and collaborated with musicians, filmmakers, and visual artists. She currently teaches at Brown University.

Your Kingdom was designed by HR Hegnauer.

Text is set in LTC Caslon and Tuppence.